IT'S ME, DULCET TONES

Half Inch Press

Other Books by Kenneth Pobo

It Gets Dark So Soon Now
At The Window, Silence
Sore Points
Lilac and Sawdust
A Vision Tested in the Flower
Uneven Steven
Wingbuds
Dindi Expecting Snow
The Antlantis Hit Parade
Loplop in a Red City
Booking Rooms in the Kuiper Belt
Bend of Quiet
Glass Garden
Introductions
Ordering: A Season in My Garden
Musings from the Porchlit Sea

IT'S ME, DULCET TONES

Kenneth Pobo

For Stan

Anniversary

Owl And Swing

DULCET TONES RAISED IN NAPERVILLE

Mom had an affair
with the Maytag repairman.
Something always broke down.
A lamp or a marriage.

The repairman was like a pill.
Mom turned her life over
to Jesus, stopped the affair
cold. Dad never found out,
never looked too hard.
He had fallen for a scoreboard
and never told my mom
though she suspected.

Suspecting is what we did.
Putting 2 + 2 together and
finding we couldn't do math
after all. We heard dreams
of a lawn sprinkler,
the bad cough of a tailpipe,
ate supper, and after
Johnny Carson, evening
put us to bed, no tucking in.

DULCET APOLOGIZES

I played Kick the Can—
until I felt sorry for the can. I carried it
from the cement road and let it rest
on my window sill with a view
of our Chinese elm tree, a magic tree,

as all trees are. I squirted the wash cloth
from the kitchen sink with dish soap
and carried it back to my room.
The can looked cleaner, even shiny,
but I had bent it up too much.
I told it secrets, a tin priest
forgiving me again

and again. I grew up, sort of,
and took the can with me.
I don't much believe in luck,
but I'm superstitious. It's not
that I fear something bad
will happen if I let go,
but I'll miss out on something good.

When I look at lit candles at night,
I miss the moon. I need it
for the many songs
only it can teach me.

DULCET AS BARRED OWL

I ask Mom, Who
cooks for you? No one,

she says. She runs her kitchen
        as she slips
deep into a flour concentration,
worshipping at the altar of spices.
This is her favorite time.

Sometimes I watch her,
but she doesn't see me
flying out the window,
perching in my tree.

OLD NEWS

As Dulcet sucks
juice from a pomegranate,
his mother tells him that he is

a blob. She laughs,
doesn't mean it. Usually.
He lobs the pomegranate

at her head. Ouch,
she says. Night shows up
at the door selling subscriptions.

Dulcet's mother tries
to convert the salesman.
No sale. Dulcet would have liked

a magazine. He reads fissures
formed a billion years ago
on the moon's surface.

Old news. It's enough.

DULCET ON A SWING

At ten my mother died. I went
to the park and swung for hours.
She was in heaven, my grandparents said—
the swing got me as close to heaven
as I could get. I always came back down,
a fried bologna sandwich by my place

when I got home. Sometimes I heard
mom's voice coming up from the basement.
It sounded like an egg cracked. She said
I should be interesting. If I swang

high enough, I'd wear cloud shorts.
I'd be interesting.

HIS DEAD MOTHER

I bought paper as blue
as bluebird eggs. My letter
included a mountain, mist
around the top, a heavy load
for the bird to haul. Birds,
up to their beaks
in miracles. I thanked you and

told you about when I
danced alone at home and a pot
slid out of the cupboard
onto my head.

You pulled me up then
(as your memory does today)
and I kept dancing.

DULCET AND PROBLEM SOLVING

The problem goes on the board.
She explains how we solve it.
I drift to the smell of baking
bread at my grandparents' house.

Her shoes fascinate me, wooden
with wooden flowers on top.
She clacks with each step.
When I fail a big test she lets me
take it again. I ace it. I have,
evidently, solved the problems.

I go home happy but problems
walk with me. Maybe if I had
her magic shoes, my problems
would become good little
equations and solve themselves.

In my bedroom I watch night,
a brown recluse, size me up.

DULCET'S YOUNGER DAYS

Oh to be 13 again when I
was ecstatic and awful.
Afternoons when my friend
and I would get naked together.
I was the pond that desire chose
to swim in. Days like yellow
rosebuds that kept opening
as if summer had come to stay.

But oh, how awful to be 13,
the first stirrings of heartbreak,
to go to school and try to be
as invisible as possible,
keeping secrets from others
and myself. When I think of

younger days I tremble
with joy, with fear.

DULCET AND PROOF

In Geometry class, shapes keep numbers
in their pockets. I didn't know how easily
numbers can explode. Mr. Grotier

in brown hushpuppies says I need
to prove that a triangle is a triangle.
I can't prove most of what I love.

A magenta aviary has colorful birds
under my eyelids. Mr. Grotier believes in
Side Side Side. I'm beside myself, a perch

dreaming up lily pads to swim under.
My yellow flower head looks up at rowboats.
A trapezoid sun leads me to a sandbar where

a pine calls an eagle to it. Intuition,
the last step of my proof. Am I crazy?
Well, that's about the size of it.

IN COMPLETE DARKNESS

At 16 Dulcet
dawdled in a swamp,
saw a log in water,
and just as his leg almost
landed on it, the gator
swam away. Just this week
he crossed train tracks
and didn't hear the train
coming. He made it,
barely. Aunt Triton told him
to pay attention. He does.
To the many houses
he sees in the eye
of a violet. To genies
that fly out from
garage windows.

He's like the moon--
while focusing on
a still pond, the killer
gets away
in complete darkness.
where even the pines are lost.

THE KISS

Dulcet crushes
on his science lab partner, Gil,
a kid with hairy legs and a good head
for science. Dulcet prefers English—
and even then he's picky.
Mythology? Yes. Shakespeare? No.

Gil does all the work and Dulcet gets half
the credit. He imagines kissing Gil
as they work on an exercise
in their *For Home, Desk, And Lab* book,
tragic pages full of horrible problems.
Gil would never kiss another boy.
Or so he says

when Dulcet, matter of factly, says
I'd like to kiss you. They never see
each other after science ends.
Gil majors in Bio, finds a girlfriend.

Dulcet has a kiss growing inside him
that's ready to explode,
his lip buds ready to bloom.

SOME BLOCKY SOPHOMORE THROWS A BASKETBALL
RIGHT AT DULCET'S HEAD

Coach sees Danny throw it
right at me—when I fall,
Coach yells get up. I want to cry
but know they'll turn me
into a bigger joke
than they think I am. Why does

Eisenhower High School make me
play basketball? Run this way,
then that, throw a ball up.
I'd rather be on the couch
watching *One Life To Live,*
Viki fading into her split
personality, Niki Smith. I feel

pretty split,
like I'm several people,
none of whom can dodge anything.

ROOMS

1. In Chapel

At 10:00 we hear about
Bolivia's heathen. Cute guys

and a hymnal, bodies
like open houses

inviting me in. Later,
I dance in secret,

begin to nudge
open my closet door

which does, at long last,
let in the light.

2. Trying to check in

A high school senior in the fall of 1971.
These were great days, I was told—
I'd never be this happy again. Maybe
happiness is a hotel room,
chocolates on the bed,
only it burns down
before I check in.

3. Passing

Aunt Stokesia asked me
ever since puberty
"When will you get a girlfriend?"
I passed

her question onto a straight
self I had invented,
and said "Someday."

Someday jumped into a fire.
I didn't try to rescue it.
I entered
the door
of a kiss,

love, a room
I'd never want to leave.

DULCET WATCHING *THE SEVENTH SEAL*

My boyfriend Roger and I are bored.
With everything. A stock market,
the sun can rise or fall. Our passion
flower vine might have
a breath-stopping bloom,
a perfect moment. One day we'll stop
breathing entirely.

In our game, I'm a knight and Roger
is death. I stink at games. He always wins.
In the red rocker he warms
cold chess pieces on his lap.

DULCET COMES OUT TO HIS UNRESPONSIVE DAD

Dad, if I tell you I'm the fig newton
in the box of raisin cookies,
will you get it then?

You're a mailbox,
a slot that can't be opened.
I'm the letter falling
on the sidewalk. Still,

I keep trying to get through--
we'll be better friends then.
The mail will arrive,
all of it.

DULCET FAILS GEOLOGY

Well, it's a rock. I know
I'll lose points
on the Lab test, but

the rock wants
no biography written
of its slowly eroding life.

My life erodes too.
I prefer a bendy world,
nothing rock solid,

elastic as a goose
neck curving around
a leaning reed.

Roses on Cold Planets

AND WAITS

Dulcet's grandmother Mitsi
called herself the toast of '46. Gentlemen
often asked her out. She wore
white gloves and corsages,
talked of this perfect necklace of time—

that ended when she married Herb,
nice enough, like a turnip on a window sill.
Mitsi thought he'd make big money.
She'd have corsages from rare
cataleya orchids. Instead she had four kids,
each like a car with something wrong
under the hood. It's like a dream
hid in the jewelry box of her life,
but the thief pulled her out anyway.

Dulcet looks for a stronger jewelry box,
hears footsteps in the hall.
The door opens—
he looks the thief in the eye
and waits.

DULCET AND MITSI

My grandmother Mitsi says
that someday I'll grow out of
being gay. I have outgrown
many things, my favorite
yellow shirt, a taste for
licorice on noodles.
But not this.
Why outgrow joy?

Mitsi says she herself hasn't
outgrown much, that she's
the same as ever. She's water
in a pot turned on to full boil.
But not always. She's also
moss roses, sun-opened,
colors spilling out.

SWEETBRIAR TONES

While Dulcet drinks lemonade
with two ice cubes, he remembers
his dad's mother, Sweetbriar Tones,
who had many talents. She could fly.

And raise the dead—
if they were willing.
Most weren't. They liked hearing
Earth's whispered love letters.
Sometimes someone dead
did return—always itching
to slide back to death.

When Sweetbriar died,
she could still fly. Dulcet waves
as she lands on a bright
red gloxinia.

ASH AND ROSES

Dulcet Tones' favorite Aunt,
Triton, began each morning
asking "Am I still here?"

He visits the cemetery often,
talks to the dead—
and not just his Aunt.
Martha, born in 1792—a pine
shades her.

Dulcet says he won't be a plot.
His plot will be finished,
all the implausible scenes,
the many poorly phrased comebacks.

He'll become the cigarette
he no longer smokes, an ash man,
dust around red roses.

DULCET AND NERVOUS WEATHER

On the first spring morning,
I'm grouchy. I told the sun
to warm me. In the yard

I saw five flies
on the back of the garage,
a winged coffee klatch.
I wasn't invited. A white
snowdrop called to me.
He had recently pushed
through cold earth to come
into bloom. I asked
was his struggle hard.
He said yes, but he'd gladly
do it again. I'm hoping

I'll come into bloom even
in nervous weather. My red
door opens to the street.
It's time that I walk there
and not turn back.

DULCET, LATE TO THE WORLD

The world invites me to
a posh party. I wear

a gold necklace and eat
whipped diamonds. The world
has elegant trees. Flowers
stand like maids and butlers.
I'm scared of who might
be here. I wander into

a quiet room. Night
sneaks in after me—
for the first time I believe in love
at first sight.

DULCET AT THE DINNER PARTY AND LATER

I'm pleased to see this sky,
like being at a dinner party
when a handsome stranger gets seated
beside me, the conversation feels
natural and maybe I'm a little bit
in love. I'm glad when the dinner
party ends since I'm getting a headache,
Champagne does that to me, so

I say goodbye to my hosts and
dining companion, chauffer night
standing by my car, angry that I haven't
given him a raise, but I get in hoping
he's sober—he might make it
to morning

DULCET BLAMING

For messing me up,
I don't blame
my parents or
their parents or
their parents.
Or Adam and Eve.
Snakes can be persuasive
when you're naked.
I don't blame the snake,
a chatty little guy.
Should I blame DNA?
A sperm and an egg
make a mess and soon
I'm in third grade,
Mrs. Olaf demanding
that I spell frostbite,
which I get wrong—
she looks like the roof
caves in on her permanent.

What is permanent?
Things keep moving away.
I follow after.

LAVENDER NUPTUALS

When Dulcet proposed to Ape, he didn't get down on
his knee because of a football injury he had in high
school. Ape wasn't sentimental anyway. They had
been a couple for two decades already.

They wed in a Universalist-Unitarian church. The
minister, who they had never met, sang "Oh Promise
Me." Three cats preened in the sanctuary. Their friend
Millie wore a huge white hat that looked like an alien
spacecraft. Dulcet wore a tuxedo. Ape wore shorts and
flip flops. They didn't fight over their choices. Why fight
the direction of the wind?

After the ceremony, Ape and Dulcet both had a martini,
unusual for them at noon, and ordered calamari, not
unusual. Routine did their laundry, but they liked
routine. They had a room for it by the broom closet.

Divorce is like a puma sneaking up behind you. Dulcet
and Ape haven't encountered it yet. They hope it
doesn't find a way into their yard. It may. They water
the dahlias, clean the garage windows.

DULCET AND APE BURP

On the lanai I read
Middlemarch. You're in the garage
reading your name written in pollen
on our Mustang. We have war

sometimes. I'm always right.
Why is that? Do I have that wrong?
Sometimes we have peace,
a venus flytrap almost ready
to close around a bug.
After many years,

we still have much in common,
jump into the same underpants
of time and chafe. We kiss, burp,
and dyspeptic dandelions stab us
with yellow knives. Someday

hungry death will open
our refrigerator. It's rude
to just walk right in.
But it's death. It can lick
any lock until it melts.

DULCET TAKES UP PAINTING

When I tell Ape
I want to be de Chirico,
he says de who? Art
makes him turn the TV up louder.
I ask what he wants for dinner.
No response. Somebody is winning
again on *Jeopardy*. I can't watch—
everything must start with a question.

I pile up questions in my back seat
and haul them to the resale shop.
Even they don't want them. Yet

my paintings will be questions
rescuing stray answers from the street.
Light will ache out of shadows
the way I ache out of sleep.
I'm maybe there, vague but alert.

I may paint Ape's portrait,
something abstract.
A remote in a chocolate cake.

DULCET AND APE PLAY RISK

Ape wants to win.
At any cost.
He captures Irkutsk,
feeds the lion
of conquest.
I keep playing
knowing I'll lose—

after driving me
from Greenland,
he rolls the dice,
this pacifist
in a rainbow sweater.

STAY AWHILE

Dulcet thinks he needs to fire
up Ape's desire. Ape buries himself
in gardening magazines, almost
forgets that Dulcet even lives
in the house. While listening

to "Stay Awhile" by The Bells from 1971,
two breathy vocalists sex out
a sexy scene, the breathy boy sings
that she drops her robe to the floor.

Dulcet dons his salmon robe,
hummingbirds on the back,
drops his robe to the floor.
Ape keeps reading. In a film,
lust would seize Ape,
like Gomez when Morticia speaks French.
This is no film. It's Tuesday

and the dishes need doing.
He goes downstairs to dirty plates
where he will stay awhile.

DULCET READS A NEW ASTRONOMY BOOK

The sun will
melt our history.
My days, fizz
of a just-poured
7-Up, my feelings
going flat.

Time
and space
will play ball,
darkness,

the only winner.

DULCET SAYS HE'S BEEN ON THE MOON

When I get to the moon
I step through a big white door,
drop on a creaky couch,

no one around, just me
and cats made of dust.
The moon mocks our spaceships,

prefers to chat with
her brother and sister,
Triton and Europa.

Back on Earth, bees of logic
sting tables and chairs.
Moonlight rubs my nape.

DULCET ON PLUTO

I go to Pluto. Imagination
faster than any rocket.
387 degrees below zero.
We bring beach blankets,
stars, psychedelic popcorn!
They resist being counted,
dislike getting herded
into an equation.

A soothing night settles around us.
Five moons fluff our pillows.

Anniversary

DULCET DREAMS OF HIS HUSBAND

When I have that dream of you again,
the one that's a little scary, a little erotic,
it dawns on me that my dreams normally
lack music. Like our marriage. I'm sure
that's not a dream. Didn't we stand
in the Unitarian Church, light coming in
through tall windows? It happened, yes?

Years stack up, leftovers. Good night,
good night, kiss. Then the dream
which I still haven't told you.

DULCET GROCERY SHOPPING

9:00 and the store is like a man
about to sneeze. Everyone waits for it.
It doesn't come so we go from aisle
to aisle, forgetting the world beyond
the electric eye and glass doors.

Time is on the shelf. I grab it and shake.
It smells funny. I see that it's not for sale
after all. I put it back—but it won't go back.
I can't return it.

Cashier Evelyn will know what to do.
She rasps out a sincere hello,
says that I'll have to take time with me.
A store policy. I toss it in a bag
with chicken wings and cherry water ice.

As I woggle my cart to my car,
I see a gray sky, like a dirty shower liner.
It was sunny when I entered.
I drive home. Time preens,
looks in the rearview mirror,
totally relaxed. It's easy to relax
when you never die.

UNSPONTANEOUS DULCET

I should open
the window
in a rainstorm,
but I worry about
warped surfaces.
Maybe I'm
a warped surface.

I begin each day
the same way—
feed the cats, pour coffee,
put on a CD. Then I'm
ready for work where
my boss considers me
a solved equation.
I don't feel solved.

Am a train about
to lose its cars,
yet I make the curve
almost.

DULCET IN PENELOPE'S DINER

At the next table
two guys talk about me.
They think they're
talking about their god.
But it's me.

The suited guy says fags
must be rounded up—
and branded.
The guy in the blue pants
says Jesus holds
the branding iron. So,

I'm cattle. I've been cattle before.
In school boys laughed
since I preferred playing
with girls. I still do.
Being unable to throw a football,
a reason to attack.

These diners would be happy
to kill me. God
insists that they do.

DULCET IN A DINER THREE DAYS BEFORE IT BURNS
DOWN UNDER SUSPICIOUS CIRCUMSTANCES

Sitting at the same booth every Wednesday, Dulcet
orders fried chicken, iced tea, and fries. This is not
negotiable. When it comes to food, Dulcet is a large
menu, everything he dislikes cut out. Henrietta, or Hen,
serves him. It must be Hen or Dulcet grabs his coat and
leaves.

Today he decides to play the jukebox at his table. It only
has old country songs. "I am an old country song," he
says to nobody. Hen is less friendly today.

The song he plays three times is by Bill Anderson and
Jan Howard: "Dissatisfied." He likes when Bill calls Jan
a dingy redhead. Dulcet is a redhead too. And
dissatisfied. Mostly with his soul. It's gotten shopworn.
He thought it was original until he saw dozens of them
in the Perkdale Resale Shop.

The fried chicken is pretty good today. The fries, a little
greasy. The iced tea, always the one thing to count on.

DULCET IN PRIVATE

Dulcet says: I'm sick from opacity.
Even a sunny day brings a shadow.
Where is wisdom? Where is sagacity?

Searching for it kills my vitality,
withers me, a hollyhock that won't grow.
Dulcet says: I'm sick from opacity

blurring vision, fading tenacity.
I wish I were quicker but I move slow.
Where is wisdom? Where is sagacity?

Sometimes I hear it in an old country
and western song. I forget the words, though.
Dulcet says: I'm sick from opacity—

Kent told his king "See better, Lear." I see
poorly so I fall for a faux hero.
Where is wisdom? Where is sagacity?

The Earth may tell me eventually.
I will follow where the river must go.
Dulcet says: I'm sick from opacity.
Where is wisdom? Where is sagacity?

DULCET PASSING TIME

My doctor tells me to
stay indoors.
Dust decorates me
like Christmas tree ornaments.

I'm having trouble
separating days.
I should color code them.
I still remember Saturday.
I was born on one. Sugar
in my coffee, the calendar
dissolves. I eat breakfast
and talk to my azure vase.
It gets sassy. And it's
only 10:00,

hours like a slow creek,
a twig caught
against a just-visible rock.

SOMETHING LEFT OUT

When I write to Dulcet Tones, I admit little,
certainly not that I killed him
and tossed the body in the Delaware River.
I keep it light, remind him of junior high
when I danced with an ostrich
named Clyde Oostervan, the music teacher
who got fired for removing all the flutes
from the sky. He thought Clyde danced well
and I was clumsy. Dulcet shouldn't talk.
He walked into a cave looking for
a fifty-cent piece and got captured
by a band of marauding salamanders.
Those were the good old days. Even
the good old days need a job. I got angry,
stabbed Dulcet Tones, and no one knew
I did it. Even Dulcet thought it was Humply Ash,
a known betrayer of the young. I enter this letter

like a bike with no rider, speed down the street,
crash into Dulcet's spirit. It's warm,
a heated marshmallow.

DULCET IN SHADE

I yen for Neptune,
to curl up in his frozen
blue arms. Moony Neptune,

the sun barely a cough.
I ought to stay with Earth,
even as we ruin it more

each day. For now,
it has flowers. I swim
in a red daylily's vast pool.

And trees. In shade
I listen to a pebble
recite her first poem.

DULCET'S STILL LIFE

Ape and he talk about
cars backfiring,

organ music, and kidney stones.
Fresh lemonade sweats

in glasses Dulcet inherited
from his grandmother.

A bowl of peaches teases
Cezanne out of the grave.

DULCET IN THE SHOWER

I can't get a song out of my head.
I'm a cave and the song echoes
throughout me, a honky tonk song
by Gary Stewart, "Ten Years of This,"
about a bad relationship. Like the one

I had with... well, someone,
vaguely human. Ten years lasted
ten seconds. When we kissed lavender
frogs popped out of our mouths.
We named them Hoppy and Happy.

I kept leaning on the everlasting
arms of now. Someone said forever.
Forever has a large room.
When I entered it, red drapes
caught on fire. Someone pulled me
out just in time. I said thank you,

preferring now more—
it smelled like baking bread.
Someone said oh and walked away.

That was a song too. Sometimes
I sing it in the shower. By the time I'm dry,
I've forgotten it.

DULCET ON GETTING AHEAD SOMEDAY

I'm in my pajamas
at 3 in the afternoon.
I haven't showered. Maybe
I did a few days ago. Sink
dishes form an army
to overthrow me. I should be
overthrown. Sometimes I sit
by the window, sure that nights
now are darker than before.
The moon turns her back on us.

I used to think I'd be getting ahead.
Someday got stuck between floors
on an elevator. Nobody to rescue it.

In the morning the clock
will aim its second hand at me,
shoot--I'll drop down,
not dead, just wounded.

DULCET ON WEDNESDAY

I do a few things well.
My mashed potatoes lack lumps,
creamy and butter-welcoming. Mostly,

I'm like Wednesday. I come around
each week, sometimes rainy,
sometimes not. The calendar
makes a space for me
like someone on a subway
moving a bit to give me room
to sit down. Thursday

waits to give me a shove.

DULCET OPENS UP

Usually I find the world scary so
I close the back and front doors.
If someone knocks, I sneak to
the basement. Last summer
a missionary tapped on
the window. I pretended
to be a manikin. Actually,

I wasn't pretending.
At work I'm in a cubicle, a box,
something removed from the box
and propped up.
I go home. Tonight I'll leave

my doors open. I'm as afraid
as ever but just this once.
Maybe I'll change
my life. I need a new language
of slam and creak.
If someone comes, I may not
let them in, but I won't
send them away.

If I like the breeze I'll open
the door even more. A dream
may stop by. I'll let it rest
in my head and make plans.

DULCET WAKING UP

Was it just a minute ago
when dreams pooled on
the avocado sheet?

I squint at origami blossoms
by our dining room window,
hold onto what's going—wind

pushes me out the door.
I squeeze between pollen
grains, the sun afraid

of rain. Even
a single drop
can make it disappear.

DULCET'S RECURRING DREAM

I watch an *I Love Lucy*
rerun that I've seen at least 50 times.
The wash slurgs in the basement.
I scrubbed a breakfast bowl. Everything's
ready for lunch. I've done this
for half a century, not knowing that

I was dreaming. I had not lived a real life.
What's a real life? One day
I'm seven years old at a Memorial Day
parade, scouts walking past.
The next day the army

breaks in, searches my house.
I'm to be questioned.
Downtown. Can my fingerprints
quickly learn how to lie? I must
have done something.

But they won't say.

DULCET ROWING

Organ notes drift through
his bedroom window—

music helps him toss logs
on an inner fire. He drifts

off under an efficient
crimson moon, rows

out to a bay of song,
drops anchor, night

a water lily fully open
that he can't see.

DULCET UNDER PRESSURE

In the vaccine line a stranger
says his son was very good
at baseball and did well
under pressure. Many fold
but not his son. I must be
someone who folds. Pressure
is like a bad sneeze. You can't
hold it back. It will be known.

As a teenager I lived
under pressure to please
don't come out.
Stay in the closet.
Gramps won't understand.
It will affect your chances
of getting a decent job.

Bowing to the pressure
invited stronger pressure.
Secrets weigh more than cars—
or wounds. Achoo!

I blurted secrets.
No more me as nail,
pressure as hammer.
Pressure never stops.
I can breathe now.
I can breathe.

Acknowledgments

433: "Dulcet on a Swing," "Dulcet Watching *The Seventh Seal*"

Alan Squire Publishing: "Dulcet on Pluto"

Backchannels: "In Complete Darkness"

Beliveau Review: "Dulcet, Late to the World"

Bombay Review: "Dulcet Comes Out to His Unresponsive Dad"

Ceresus Magazine: "Dulcet Writes to His Dead Mother," "Dulcet in Penelope's Diner," "Dulcet Passing" (from "Rooms")

Chiron Review: "Lavender Nuptuals"

Feed: "Dulcet in the Shower"

Gnashing Teeth: "Something Left Out"

Great Weather for Media: "Dulcet Grocery Shopping"

Home Planet News: "Old News" (as "It's Enough"), "And Waits," "Dulcet and Ape Burp"

Inkwell: "Dulcet at the Dinner Party and Later"

In Parenetheses: "Dulcet's Younger Days," "Dulcet Passing Time," "Dulcet Waking Up," "Dulcet Rowing"

Io: "Dulcet's Recurring Dream"

Iris: "Dulcet in Private"

Mockingheart Review: "Dulcet Apologizes"

Morning Fruit: "Dulcet on Wednesday"

Neon Mariposa: "Dulcet as Barred Owl," "Dulcet on Getting Ahead Someday"

Overneath Books: "Dulcet Opens Up"

Paper Dragon: "Unspontaneous Dulcet"

Peeking Cat: "Dulcet and Proof," Dulcet's Still Life"

Pine Cone Review: "Dulcet Dreams of His Husband"

Pittsburgh Poetry Journal: "The Kiss"

Plainsongs: "Dulcet Blaming"

Pocket Fiction: "Dulcet Fails Geology"

The Q&A Queer Zine: "Dulcet and Nervous Weather"

Quiver Review: "Dulcet Under Pressure"
Ran Off with the Star Bassoon: "Dulcet in a Diner Three Days Before It Burns Down Under Suspicious Circumstances"
Rat's Ass Journal: "Some Blocky Sophomore Throws a Basketball at Dulcet's Head"
Retirement Plan: "Dulcet Trying to Check-in" (from "Rooms")
RK Winter: "Dulcet Reads a New Astronomy Book"
Rockvale Review: "Dulcet Takes Up Painting"
The Rush: "Ash and Roses"
Sin Fronteras: "Dulcet Tones Raised in Naperville"
Spotlong Review: "Stay Awhile"
The Stray Bunch: "Dulcet and Problem Solving," "Sweetbriar Tones"
TAB: The Journal of Poetry and Poetics: "Dulcet in Chapel" (from "Rooms")
Taj Mahal Review: "Dulcet and Mitsi"
Tether's End: "Dulcet Says He's Been on the Moon"

Cover art: Matt Morris

About the Author

Kenneth Pobo (he/him) lives in Pennsylvania with his husband. For thirty-three years he taught English and creative writing at Widener University. He is the author of thirty-three chapbooks and fifteen full-length collections. Recent books include *Bend of Quiet* (Blue Light Press), *At the Window, Silence* (Fernwood Press), *Lilac and Sawdust* (Meadowlark Press), and *Lavender Fire, Lavender Rose* (BrickHouse Books). His work has appeared in *North Dakota Quarterly, Amsterdam Review, The Fiddlehead, Nimrod, Grain, Indiana Review, Mudfish, Hawaii Review,* and elsewhere.

www.ingramcontent.com/pod-product-compliance
Lightning Source LLC
Chambersburg PA
CBHW061803050726
47598CB00002B/850